You Are One
Amazing Lady

You Are One
Amazing Lady

*Special thoughts to
share with a truly
wonderful woman*

D. Pagels

Blue Mountain Press™
Boulder, Colorado

Library of Congress Control Number: 2013939019
ISBN: 978-1-59842-758-5

█ and Blue Mountain Press are registered in U.S. Patent and Trademark Office.
Certain trademarks are used under license.

Printed in China.
First Printing: 2013

✺ This book is printed on recycled paper.

This book is printed on paper that has been specially produced to be acid free (neutral pH) and contains no groundwood or unbleached pulp. It conforms with the requirements of the American National Standards Institute, Inc., so as to ensure that this book will last and be enjoyed by future generations.

Blue Mountain Arts, Inc.
P.O. Box 4549, Boulder, Colorado 80306

So many of the smiles in my heart are there... because of you.

I want you to think of those smiles every time you see this book... and in all the days to come. You are someone who is very special to me.

And you always will be.

I want you to know that you're one amazing lady.

You are so good to the people in your life. So considerate and caring. When you give, it's easy to see that it comes straight from the heart... and it gives everyone around you the gift of a nicer world to live in...

I hope you'll never forget how much I treasure just being in this world with you. And I love knowing that everyone else feels the same way I do. To your friends, you are everything a friend should be. To your family, I know you are dearly loved and truly the best.

You are such a deserving person.
And I really hope that all your
days are as beautiful and as
bright... as the ones you inspire
in other people's lives.

Not All Angels
Have Wings

Not all angels have wings. But they're angels... all the same. You can tell who they are by the way they make everyone around them feel more hopeful and happy and more at peace... and the way they make everything in life a little more complete.

I don't have all the perfect words to express how important you are to me, but I want you to remember that you're an every-day angel to me, and I truly don't know what I'd ever do without you.

I am beyond lucky to have you in my life... and I'm so glad you're here!

Beautiful Things
That Are True About You

You are something — and someone — very special. You really are. No one else in this entire world is exactly like you, and there are so many beautiful things about you.

You're a one-of-a-kind treasure, uniquely here in this space and time. You are here to shine in your own wonderful way, sharing your smile in the best way you can, and remembering all the while that a little light somewhere makes a little more radiance everywhere...

You can — and you do — make a wonderful contribution to this world.

You have qualities within you that many people would love to have, and those who really and truly know you... are so glad that they do.

You have a big heart and a good
and sensitive soul. You are gifted
with thoughts and ways of seeing
things that only special people know.
You know that life doesn't always play
by the rules but that, in the long run,
everything will work out...

You understand that you and your actions are capable of turning anything around — and that joys once lost can always be found. There is a resolve and an inner reserve of strength in you that few ever get to see. You have so many treasures within — those you're only beginning to discover... and all the ones you're already aware of.

*Never forget what a treasure you
are. That special person in the mirror
may not always get to hear all the
compliments you so sweetly deserve,
but you are so worthy
    of such an abundance...
        of friendship, joy, and love.*

I think you are unaware of how extraordinary you are and how exquisite you will always be.

There's a very good reason why this book for you is filled with flowers. It's because everything blossoms a little bit more in your presence.

And one of the things that touches my heart the most... is just knowing that any day with you in it... is going to be a lovely day.

A Little Story About "You and Me"

Me: So lucky to have this special connection!

You: The wonderful person I'm so thankful for.

Me: Someone who means well, but doesn't always get it right.

You: Someone who gives my life so much assurance and encouragement.

Me: A little insecure, a little uncertain, a little crazy sometimes.

You: A huge help and a calming influence... all the time.

You: Know what's going on inside me
better than anyone.

Me: There isn't anybody else I can trust
like this and no one I feel so
comfortable turning to.

You: On a scale of 1 to 10, with 10 being
the best, at least a 20.

Me: Counting my blessings and hearing
your name come up so many times.

You: A joy to be with, to think of, and
just to talk to.

Me: So incredibly glad... there's you.

A List of Your Superpowers
(some of the special things about you)

You're so fantastic! One smile from you can really improve the whole day ❧ It always seems like you can be everywhere at once: one minute you're on my mind, the next minute you're very tenderly in my heart ❧

You are awesome at boosting everyone's spirits with your great attitude, your encouragement and understanding, and your willingness to reach out with an amazing amount of love ≼ That's just the way you are ≼ You give life a gleam that most people only carry a glimpse of...

Every day you manage to go a million miles out of your way to make things nicer for the people in your life ⬿ *You're great at bouncing right back from any adversity, and you're an inspiration to so many people in so many ways* ⬿ *You seem to see right through to the solution to problems, and you're always happy to lend a helping hand* ⬿

You're so unassuming about all the remarkable things you've done and the impressive things you do, but the fact of the matter is this: you're nothing short of amazing ⇐ What you give us all is a really special gift ⇐

And to tell you the truth... "super" doesn't even begin to cover it ⇐

May You Be Blessed
with All These Things

A little more joy,
a little less stress,
a lot more understanding
of your wonderfulness.

Abundance in your life,
blessings in your days,
dreams that come true,
and hopes that stay.

Friendship in many faces,
love in all its forms,
safe journeys, true success,
and sweet rewards.

Courage with its strength,
serenity with its calm,
the ability to always
hang in there and carry on.

A rainbow on the horizon,
an angel by your side,
and everything
that could ever bring
a smile to your life.

Do You Know How Important You Are to Me?

*I know you probably wonder from time
to time what you mean to me.
So I'd like to share this thought with you,
to tell you that you mean the world to me.*

*Think of something you couldn't live without...
and multiply it by a hundred.*

*Think of what happiness means to you...
and add it to the feelings you get on
the best days you've ever had.*

*Add up all your best feelings and take
away all the rest... and what you're
left with is exactly how I feel
about you.*

*You matter more to me than you can
imagine and much more than I'll
ever be able to explain.*

You have given me so many gifts, but there is one that is the nicest of all...

*you have given me
so much to be thankful for.*

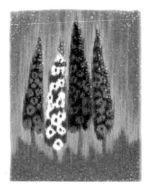

Thank you for all the happiness you bring. Thank you for all the good feelings you've inspired and all the meaningful things you do.

I would love it if everyone knew how much there is to appreciate about you!

You usually know exactly how I feel about everything, but there's something I want you to know for sure:

I think you're one of the nicest treasures anyone, anywhere... could ever ask for.

Your Presence Is a Present to the World

If it weren't for you, I wouldn't have as much hope and encouragement... or nearly as much joy. I wouldn't have as much peace and understanding. And I definitely wouldn't have as much fun!

I love that you're here. And whether it's in person or on the phone... I love the connection that is always there between us.

I feel so much more at home with you than I do with most people. And the moments we share are some of the most precious times I will ever have. You endear yourself to me in so many ways.

What a splendid present — and what a beautiful presence — you are. It's a little slice of heaven on earth... having you here.

There Are Stars Above
and Stars Below

I think it's true that people are a little bit like stars. There are millions of them to see, but there are always a few that outshine all the others.

The people who warm your heart and lift up your life... those are the kind you want to have around you. Those are the ones you just adore.

Of all the stars there are, you are one of the most radiant. You give a special glow to a lot of people's lives, and you are thanked more than you'll ever know... for all the warmth and happiness you bring.

So Touched by You

Inside of me there is a place... where my sweetest dreams reside, where my highest hopes are kept alive, where my deepest feelings are felt, and where my favorite memories are tucked away, safe and warm.

My heart is a lasting source of serenity.
Only the most special things in my world
get to come inside and stay there forever.

And every time I get in touch with the
hopes, feelings, and memories in my
heart, I realize how deeply my life has
been touched by you.

You have always seemed to me like one of the most unique and remarkable people I will ever have the pleasure of knowing.

You could never give me a more
precious gift than just being in my life
and making so many moments more
gratifying than my words can say.

What you are each and every day
of your life is what you will always
and forever be.

You're absolutely cherished by me.

It takes someone special to do what you do. It takes someone rare and remarkable to make the lives of everyone around them better and more abundant.

It takes someone who has a big heart and a caring soul. It takes someone who is living proof of how precious a person can be.

It takes someone... just like you.

I Admire So Much
About You

I admire the life that you lead and the kindness that is such a sweet and natural part of you.

I admire the way you treat other people.

I admire how easily a smile finds its way to your face.

I admire the work that you do and the places your journeys take you.

I admire your dedication to all the right things and your devotion to your friends and your family.

I admire how completely you care and how you are always there for the people who need you.

I admire you with all my heart for being the hope and delight that you are to my life.

When I don't have the perfect words to tell you how much you're appreciated, I feel like you can look right into my heart... and understand. And when I'm trying to say how thankful I am for you and tears come to my eyes, you know they have nothing to do with sadness... and everything to do with joy.

There aren't many people who have a one-in-a-million person in their life... like I do. And if I made a list of all the admirable qualities you have, it would reach all the way to the moon and back.

Just like my feelings for you.

Gifts I Wish I Could Give You

The gift of knowing that it's people like you who make life so sweet... for people like me.

All your friends and loved ones, from close by and miles away, warming your heart in some special way.

Days that shine so bright and
wishing stars that come out at night
to listen to everything your heart is
hoping for.

Paths ahead that take you to all the
places you want to be and that bring
you closer to all the great things
you deserve.

And happiness that simply overflows...
from memories made, peacefulness
within, and the anticipation of so
many good things to come.

Everyone Should Have Someone Amazing in Their Life...

And I can think of so many reasons why that person — for me — will always be you.

You're a breath of fresh air in my days. You're a safe, sharing, understanding place I can turn to.

You're a sanctuary I can take refuge in... and someone I know I can trust with anything.

I love that you accept me as I am, that you see the world the same way I do, and that you know the way to my heart so easily.

I love that I always feel happier when I know I'm going to talk to you. And I always feel so lucky and more at peace after I do.

Everyone needs someone who is always there and always caring...

*Everyone needs someone who is just a
touch or a card or a phone call away —
someone with whom you can share
everything that's in your heart or simply
talk about the day in the way that only the
two of you can.*

*Everyone needs someone to encourage
them, to believe in them, to give a pat on
the back when things have gone right
and a shoulder to cry on when they haven't.*

*Everyone needs someone to remind them
to keep trying and that it will all work out.*

*I hope everyone has someone
who is as marvelous as you.*

You will always be so many invaluable things
to me.

You are my role model extraordinaire. You
are my source of sage advice. You are my
wise counsel for some of the best things
I've learned about life.

You are a favorite traveling companion,
smiling beside me on the way to all
my tomorrows.

*You are a guardian angel with hidden wings.
You are the best support system imaginable.*

*You are wide-open arms and easy grins.
You are a come-on-in-and-make-yourself-
comfortable kind of soul. I always know I
can relax and let my guard down with you.*

*You are so many of the things I love to see
in a person... and I admire you tremendously.*

If I Could Have
a Wish Come True...

*I would wish for
nothing but magnificent things
to come to you.*

In your life, which is so precious to me,
may troubles, worries, and problems
never linger; may they only make you
that much stronger and able and wise.

And may you rise each day with sunlight
in your heart, success in your path,
answers to your prayers,
    and that smile
        — that I love to see —
          always there... in your eyes.

I'm Glad This World Has People in It Who Are as Wonderful as You

There are millions of people on this planet who would consider themselves blessed beyond belief to have a treasure like you in their lives.

And I am so glad... that I do.

*When I need a hug that lasts long enough
to enfold me with hope and acceptance
and care, I know that's the only kind
you give.*

*Any difficult day can swing completely the
other way when you are in it.*

*A talk with you can warm my heart, bring
me so much gratitude, and chase any
clouds away...*

Of all the amazing qualities you possess, just being incredibly special is one of your best traits.

It all seems to come so naturally to you... to bring so much that is so good into the lives of those around you.

There are very few people who are as impressive as you are.

*And I'm not exaggerating when I say...
if more people were like you, this world
would be a kinder, nicer, happier... and
much better place.*

What a Pleasure It Is to Have You in My Life

If you could see yourself reflected in my eyes, you would see someone who makes my heart just smile inside. You would catch a glimpse of somebody who has been such a positive influence on my life and who keeps on making a very meaningful difference in my days.

If you could hear the words I would love to share, you would be able to listen to a moving tribute to you, one that sings your praises, speaks of an unending gratitude, and describes how much I'll always appreciate you.

If you could imagine one of the nicest gifts anyone could ever receive, you would begin to understand what your presence in my life has meant to me.

You're my definition of a special person.

I think you're fantastic.
And exceptional and unique
*   and endearing.*
To me, you're someone who is
*   very necessary to my well-being.*

In so many ways, you fill my life
with happiness and the sweet feelings
of being so grateful that you're here.

I could go on and on...
   but you get the picture.

I think you're a masterpiece.

For You

I don't know exactly what it is... but there is something <u>very special</u> about you.

It might be all the things I see on the surface: Things that everyone notices and admires about you. Qualities and capabilities. Your wonderful smile, tenderly connected to a warm and loving heart. It might be all the things that set you apart from everyone else.

Maybe it's the obvious things: The way you never hesitate to go a million miles out of your way to do what's right. The way your todays help set the stage for so many beautiful tomorrows. Or maybe it's these things: Words shared heart-to-heart. An unspoken understanding. Sharing seasons. Making some very wonderful memories. The joys of two people just being on the same page in each other's history...

If I could ever figure out all the magic that makes you so special, I'd probably find out that it's a combination of all these things — blended together with the best this world has to offer: friendship and love, dreams come true, strong feelings, gentle talks, listening, laughing, and simply knowing someone whose light shines brighter than any star.

You really are amazing.

*And I feel very lucky
to have been given
the gift of knowing
how special
you are.*

What I Love About You

I can't think of a single thing I would change about you!

You are as good as it gets, and I am grateful for every moment I get to spend in the company of someone so great.

You're a generous soul and probably the most understanding person I've ever known. You may try to play it down, but you just can't... you are such an outstanding human being.

I have an immense amount of respect for you. You are filled with grace and sincerity, and you are worthy of all the praise I can send your way.

There are no words for me to describe what a joy it is for me to know you. There are a million things about you that I love.

And I just thought that would be a really nice thing... to remind you of.

There are a few absolute gems in this world. They are the people who make a tremendous difference in other people's lives... with the smiles they give, the compassion they show, and the way they warm the hearts of everyone around them.

Those unselfish and adorable people
are so deserving of every hope and
wish. They are the people who are
incredibly unique, enormously thanked,
and endlessly appreciated for everything
they do.

And one of those wonderful,
deserving, and one-of-a-kind people
is most definitely... you.

A Simple Thank-You

*O*ver the course of my life, I have
acquired a few jewels of wisdom.

I have learned that the little things
in life are really the big things.

Nicest of all are the kind words and good deeds that bring help and happiness to others.

The tenderhearted things that people do — quite often quietly, behind the scenes — lift us all up a little higher.

I need to thank you for all the days you make everything blossom more beautifully... and all the ways you raise people's spirits...

Just by being here and sharing so much of your optimism and creativity and kindness... you chase a lot of worries away and help people see a path that leads to a little more serenity.

I know you would be a little embarrassed by compliments that are too mushy or over-the-top. But there are so many moments when I wish I could say a very special thanks to you.

So I'll keep this simple... and I'll keep it sweet.

I just hope you know how very grateful I am... and how appreciated you'll always be.

It *takes a certain kind of person to be special.*

*It takes someone who is really refreshing,
someone who lights up this little corner of
the world with feelings of friendship and love
and understanding. It takes a truly unique
personality and a knack for making each day
on the calendar... a good day.*

It takes someone who's willing to put forth the energy and make the time. It takes an individual who is able to open up and share their innermost feelings with another. It takes someone who makes the journey of life easier and more rewarding. It takes a rare combination of many qualities.

It takes a certain kind of person to be special.

It takes someone... exactly like you.

*Y*ou are the gold standard that all people should be measured by.

You are such a superb example of how to live a life that enhances the happiness of everyone around you.

You are a steady stream of support, a reassuring feeling that is always with me, and a gift whose value is immeasurable. You are lovely in more ways than you know, and you always will be.

*You know this, right? That forever
I will have a smile in my heart that
belongs to you?*

Good. I knew you knew.

*Thank you for being a whole bouquet
of beautiful things that always adds to
my life. Thank you for your warm,
big-hearted way of being in the world.*

I hope you have a charmed life filled with joyful insights and new adventures, and a little divine guidance by your side. I hope you never run out of wishes and that every one you make comes true.

May you always remember that it's people like you who are celebrated so much... by people like me.

There Are So Many Things
I Treasure About You

I love that there are so many amazing things about you! I love that I feel so connected with you and that we share such a special bond. I love realizing that some things are just too wonderful for words... and my appreciative feelings for you are in that category.

I love that I get to wake up every morning in a world that has people like you in it.

May the Years to Come
Be Filled with
All These Things...

An abundance of happiness.
Blessings that warm your life
and make you smile.
Friends and loved ones by your side...
people who are going to treasure every
memory they get to make with you.
Wonderful surprises in your life.

Beautiful sunrises in your days.
Opportunities that come along.
Chances you've hoped for.
Goals you've been striving to reach.
Changes you've wanted to make.
A song in your heart.
A wish that comes true.
And reminders of how much nicer
*   this world is... all because of you.*

I wish I had a thousand ways to tell you how much you're appreciated.

Thank you for all the sweet, generous, and awesome ways you contribute to my life. You're such an important part of my days!

*So many of the good feelings in my heart
are there... because of you.*

*You've been caring and supportive every
step of the way. You're the best there is
at raising my spirits when they start to
sink, and you're always there with an
understanding heart to hear what I have
to say — and an encouraging attitude
to inspire me...*

You help me remember what's good and forget what's bad, and you always know the perfect solutions to see me through any roller-coaster moments I manage to have.

The easy thing for me to do... would just be to tell you that you're beautiful inside and out. That is — in fact — very true. But what I really want to add to that deeply personal thought is this...

You are delightful and wonderful and simply the best.

And because I have you in my life,
I am joyful
and thankful...

and incredibly blessed.

You Really Are One
Amazing Lady

Don't ever forget that. You are the kind of person everyone would love to have in their life!

You're the type of person who makes a very special difference, and you give so many people a reason to smile.

You deserve to receive the best
in return, and one of my heart's
favorite hopes is that the happiness
you give away will come back
to warm you...

each and every day
of your life.

About the Author

Best-selling author and editor Douglas Pagels has inspired millions of readers with his insights and his anthologies. His books have sold over 3 million copies, and he is one of the most quoted contemporary writers on the Internet today. Reflecting a philosophy that is perfect for our times, Doug has a wonderful knack for sharing his thoughts and sentiments in a voice that is so positive and understanding we can't help but take the message to heart.

His writings have been translated into over a dozen languages due to their global appeal and inspiring outlook on life, and his work has been quoted by many worthy causes and charitable organizations.

He and his wife live in Colorado, and they are the parents of children in college and beyond. Over the years, Doug has spent much of his time as a classroom volunteer, a youth basketball coach, an advocate for local environmental issues, a frequent traveler, and a craftsman, building a cabin in the Rocky Mountains.